FREE GIFT FOR YOU!

30-Day All-Access Trial Membership:

Contact Any Celebrity

www.ContactAnyCelebrity.com

Your #1 Source for Accurate Celebrity Contact Information

($30.00 Value!)

Activate Your Free 30-Day Trial Membership:

www.contactanycelebrity.com/free

You'll Get Instant Access To:

Our Easy-To-Use Searchable Database
The Best Mailing Addresses For Over 55,000 Celebrities Worldwide
Agent, Manager, Publicist, and Production Company Info
Phone & Fax Numbers with Email Addresses
Celebrity Charitable Causes
Daily Real-Time Updates
Free Research Requests
Postage Refund Guarantee
Toll-Free 24/7 Customer Service
Celebrity Gift Bag Opportunities
Plus Much More!

Activate Your Free 30-Day Trial Membership:

www.contactanycelebrity.com/free

Additional Resources

Books by Jordan McAuley

The Celebrity Black Book
Over 55,000 Accurate Celebrity Addresses for Fans, Businesses and Nonprofits
www.CelebrityBlackBook.com

Secrets to Contacting Celebrities
101 Ways to Reach the Rich and Famous
www.SecretsToContactingCelebrities.com

Databases

Celebrity Causes Database
www.CelebCauses.com

Contact Any Celebrity
www.ContactAnyCelebrity.com

Toolkits

Celebrity Book Endorsements Toolkit
www.BookEndorsements.com

How to Hire a Celebrity
www.HowToHireACelebrity.com

Make Your Book Famous
www.MakeYourBookFamous.com

How to Contact Celebrities for Fun and Profit:
Or How to Get Celebrity Autographs, Product Endorsements, Media Interviews, Charitable Donations and More!

Mega Niche Media LLC
8721 Santa Monica Blvd. #431
W. Hollywood, CA 90069-4507
310-388-6084 (Phone)
310-388-6084 (Fax)
www.MegaNiche.com

Visit Contact Any Celebrity (www.ContactAnyCelebrity.com) to search our online database of over 55,000 celebrities and public figures worldwide. You'll find the best mailing address, agent, manager, publicist, and production company with phone, fax, and email addresses.

ATTENTION: Quantity discounts are available on bulk purchases of this book for reselling, educational purposes, subscription incentives, gifts or fundraising. Special books or book excerpts can also be created to fit specific needs. For more information, contact our Special Sales Department at Mega Niche Media LLC, 8721 Santa Monica Blvd. #431, W. Hollywood, CA 90069.

Although the author and publisher have made every effort to ensure the accuracy and completeness of the information contained in this book, we assume no responsibility for errors, inaccuracies, omissions, or any inconsistency herein. Any slight of people, places or organizations is unintentional.

Manufactured in the United States of America
ISBN 978-1-60487-000-8

Jordan McAuley with Tsufit:
How to Contact Celebrities for Fun and Profit

Host:

Tsufit
Secrets from the Spotlight!
www.SecretsFromTheSpotlight.com

Guest Expert:

Jordan McAuley
Contact Any Celebrity
8721 Santa Monica Blvd. #431
W. Hollywood, CA 90069
310-691-5466 (Phone)
310-362-8771 (Fax)
jordan@contactanycelebrity.com
www.ContactAnyCelebrity.com

Tsufit: Hello everyone and welcome to *Secrets from the Spotlight*, the show where we go behind the scenes to get the inside scoop on how you can get noticed. I am your host, Tsufit. Today, we have a fabulous guest for you. I am so excited. Wait until you hear about this guy!

Have you ever fantasized about being able to get in touch with Al Pacino, Halle Berry, Quentin Tarantino, Sarah Jessica Parker, or LL Cool J? Here is the guy who can help you do it. Jordan McAuley, welcome to the show.

Jordan: Hi! Thanks for having me.

Tsufit: My pleasure. Folks, this guy is the real deal. He works out of Hollywood and has been on CNN. Jordan, fill us in and give us a little background. How did you get to the point that you can put me in touch with Johnny Depp? You can, right?

Jordan: Sure. I started out collecting autographs when I was in middle school and high school. It was just a hobby.

Tsufit: Where did you grow up?

Jordan: I grew up in Atlanta, Georgia and always loved celebrities and Hollywood. I was doing it as a hobby when I was around thirteen. I have always been an entrepreneur. One day, it clicked that maybe I could start selling what I knew in terms of getting celebrities' contact information and make a little extra money. When you are in high school, you need money.

Tsufit: Oh, yes. So how did you get that stuff?

Jordan: I found a list one day in the back of a magazine. This was a long time ago. I do not remember which magazine.

Tsufit: It was *Tiger Beat,* just confess.

Jordan: Probably *Tiger Beat*. It was something along the line of *Star* and *Us Weekly* that we have today.

Tsufit: Yes.

Jordan: It probably was *Tiger Beat* or one of those other magazines.

Tsufit: May I confess? If I can confess, you can.

Jordan: I cannot believe you know the name *Tiger Beat*.

Tsufit: Oh, yes. So you found some addresses and started collected them.

Jordan: I found some addresses and started putting them together in my own file. I knew then that you cannot copyright addresses, so I wasn't worried about taking and using them. As I wrote to celebrities, I would update my list of which addresses did not work and which ones did work. I started doing my own research by making my own phone calls. I basically just grew the list into a pretty big directory and started selling it by mail for about $50 each. I was making good money at the time.

Tsufit: Wow. Move over, Bill Gates.

Jordan: No. When you are in high school and you have no money, it beats working. Although I did work after-school jobs too but it beats working at Pizza Hut.

Tsufit: Oh, yes. It was McDonald's for me. If there is time to lean, there is time to clean. You missed all that.

Jordan: I started making money and got this bug of trying to do more and sell more. Some online services, like Prodigy and AOL were just starting back then so I started selling them online but this was before the real Internet like we know it today.

Tsufit: Yes. Okay, and you ended up in Hollywood.

Jordan: Right. Well, that was awhile after. I went to college at University of Miami and then film school. That is when I really realized that there was a need for this beyond just autographs. In film school, a lot of people are talking about it. I want to ask this actor to make an appearance in my student film or I want to try to get my film sent to this celebrity's production company. Everybody was looking for a job.

Tsufit: Spielberg, yes.

Jordan: Students were saying I want to write Steven Spielberg a letter so that when I graduate, maybe I can intern with him but I do not know where to reach him. I already had this list and so I started thinking, this is another way for me to go. The Internet had just boomed around '96. I bought some books on how to create a web site and I had a computer in my dorm room. There was no high speed, we all had dial-up. I created a web site (www.ContactAnyCelebrity.com) and started selling my list on the Internet, which is when it went kind of crazy because so many people started ordering and you could advertise and get traffic.

Tsufit: That is very interesting. Let me just interrupt you here. We will hear more of your story as we go. You are saying that people were tracking you down like autograph hunters and film students. Our listeners are primarily entrepreneurs, authors, speakers, some performers, business owners, CEOs, and we might even have a plumber listening. Why would they want to contact a celebrity?

Jordan: It is funny you ask that because when I tell people what I do, everybody says, "I do not really want to write a celebrity." Not everybody but there are many people, especially my parents say 'Why would you do that?"

Tsufit: Yes. My parents still do not get what I do either.

Jordan: They do not get it. They do not understand. I have realized in the last couple of years, when you have a business, it is really getting hard to stand out among the competition unless you have a celebrity attached to you. It does not have to be Jessica Simpson. You do not have to Proactiv.

Tsufit: She is one of the Simpsons, right?

Jordan: I am sorry?

Tsufit: You said Jessica. She is one of the Simpsons, right?

Jordan: Oh, yes. No. Sometimes…

Tsufit: You have to laugh at my joke, okay? It is part of the deal.

Jordan: Now, you need to have a celebrity attached to you whether you own a restaurant, you could advertise a celebrity came in there one day. Some people even have autographs or just photos of celebrities on their walls. This is just an example that you really need a celebrity attached to you somehow. Especially if you are an entrepreneur or an author, you want to have quotes from celebrities on the cover of your book. It does not have to be Tom Cruise. It does not have to be Julia Roberts but someone that has something to do with your book, maybe a local expert, a local celebrity, or another author. There are a lot of things you can do but it is not just for autograph collectors.

Tsufit: So you can put people in touch with these celebrities?

Jordan: Right. We have an online database at www.ContactAnyCelebrity.com and we basically provide contact information for almost every celebrity in the world.

Tsufit: Wow. Am I in there?

Jordan: I will let you know.

Tsufit: Soon. Jordan, the weird thing is that you and I have so much in common. When I was back in University, I did not really think about it but by the time I was 19, I had asked Donald Sutherland out for breakfast. I had asked Carol Baker, she is a country singer, if I could be her backup singer. I asked Joan Rivers if I could be on her show. Somehow, I managed to make contact but you know what? The thing a lot of people do not think about is what they should prepare before approaching a celebrity. What should you think about, Jordan, before they pick up your book? By the way, he has a book and we will tell you about that later. What should we think about before approaching a celebrity?

Jordan: What do you mean? Approaching them by mail or do you mean approaching them in person?

Tsufit: However you approach them. Let's say we get your book or your service and we know how to get in contact with a celebrity, right? Is there anything that we should think about before we write to Julia Roberts or call her, or whatever we do with it?

Jordan: Right. It depends on what you are working on. If you are an author, if you are nonprofit, you really want to think about what you are trying to get. We get letters, sometimes people think that they are supposed to write us to write the celebrities. We get letters all the time addressed to Julia Roberts and sometimes we would read them and it is amazing. Even professional organizations, like nonprofits and bigger businesses, we get these letters and they go on and on but they never really say what they want.

Tsufit: That is what I was getting at.

Jordan: A lot of them say, "Can you help me? Any help is appreciated." What do you want? Do you want them to send you an autograph that you can auction it off at a silent auction or an autograph auction? This is a great way for nonprofits or even schools or any kind of association to raise money by using celebrities. Do you want them to call a child that you have in your program that is sick? What do you want?

You have to very specific and say what you are looking for because these people are busy. The assistants that will probably look at your letter first before they pass it on to the star are busy. They get so much fan mail. Honestly, I worked at three agencies and some are production companies. They do look at the mail. A lot of people think, "Oh, they do not even look at it. They just throw that stuff away" or "It never gets to them." It is not true. It does get to them. You have to make your package when you send it stand out. We do not recommend sending packages because sometimes, especially after 9/11, there is a lot of security staff at the studios and at the production companies. Sometimes, they will just return big packages. If you want to send it, probably get a big envelope and make it look professional, even if you are just a fan looking for an autograph. Make it look professional, type it, put labels on it, and write your letter on letterhead.

Handwritten letters are not that great because people do not want to sit there and try and read it. They will glimpse at it and if they cannot read it, they are just going to throw it away. Be very short and very succinct about what you are looking for.

For example, if you are an author and you are looking for a testimonial, you might want to send it FedEx. You may want to send it UPS, not necessarily overnight, the most expensive way because that would get really expensive. When the envelope arrives at the company and it is FedEx'ed, the assistants are going to think, "Oh, this is important". They are definitely going to look at it and then, if it is a typed letter and if you enclosed postage for the return envelope. What a lot of people do is they will put in the letter "Please send me a testimonial" or "an autograph for our nonprofit." Here is our FedEx account number so then, whoever is answering the letter can just send it back FedEx using your account number. You want to make it as easy as possible is what I am trying to get at. You do not want them to have to spend any money even though a lot of people think, "Oh, they are rich and they can, it does not matter" because they are not going to do it.

Tsufit: You bring out so many fabulous points I do not know where to start. Your point about knowing what you want, I remember seeing an episode of *The Apprentice* a few years ago. The task was to put together a celebrity experience. The Trumpster had already given them contacts, so that was not the issue. But once they made contact with the celebrities, they did not know what they wanted from them.

They are standing there exactly like you said, "If there is any help you can give me" and the clock is ticking, "Well, what do you want?" You know that old thing, 'if you know what you want, you are more likely to get it'. That is really fabulous advice. What about having a fallback position if they say no to your original suggestion? I would think that might be a good idea, too. Let us say you ask for a celebrity to come into town and make a guest appearance and they say no, wouldn't it make sense to give them another down-sell as they say in marketing? Another option?

Jordan: Yes, definitely. Many of the nonprofits that we work with say in their letter, "We would love for you to make an appearance at our event" and they will describe that and give more details and the contact information for the person in-charge. They will say, "If you are not able to travel, we would at least like to get an autographed photo or piece of memorabilia we can auction off."

It is sort of like marketing. A celebrity sees it and says, "I cannot travel. I am too busy. I am shooting a film right now" or "I am on tour but here, send them an autographed script or send them an autographed guitar pick". You are probably going to get something nicer if you give them a big option first that they cannot do but then they are more likely to send you something else. "Oh, wow. We got an autographed script from so and so who is on a TV show, from Ashton Kutcher. He could not come to our event but he sent us an autographed script". You are definitely right in that respect.

Tsufit: My kids like Ashton Kutcher. How do you decide whom you would want to approach for a particular project or event? If you are an entrepreneur, how do you figure out who would be good to approach? They get your Celebrity Black Book (www.CelebrityBlackBook.com), which we will tell people about later. There are 50,000 names in it or whatever. How do you decide whom?

Jordan: The celebrity really needs to match what you are working on. If you are an entrepreneur and you have written a book on how to make money. A quote from Julia Roberts that is great but that is probably not going to help sell your book. Julia Roberts has tons of money but she is not known as somebody that is trying to make money. A quote from Donald Trump would be amazing and he has been known to actually write quotes for a lot of author's books, surprisingly. It is amazing.

Tsufit: For people who are not known? For people he had not heard of before?

Jordan: There was someone actually. I was reading about this in the PMA, Publishers Marketing Association newsletter. There was somebody who had never met him and did not know him. He made a couple of calls to his office, and just kept bugging him which you have to do sometimes especially with the bigger people. You need to do it in a polite way. You are not really bugging him, you are bugging his assistant, his secretary, whoever is answering the phone but he did.

Donald Trump sent a quote and this person was able to use it. I think it was a book on real estate. This was someone who has had success in real estate. He was not a first time author writing about something he did not really know about. He was an expert in his local real estate field but Donald Trump wrote him a testimonial.

What you have to understand is every time these quotes appear on the cover of a book, that is just better publicity and Donald Trump loves publicity. If there is a book that he says, "This is about real estate and this is someone who is really well known in Atlanta in terms of real estate. A lot of people are going to be seeing his book at book signings or at a bookstore or on his website and my name is going to be on the front. That is just more publicity for Donald Trump. So in a way, they are not doing it out of the kindness of their hearts. People think, "Oh, why are they going to take the time to send me an endorsement?"

Tsufit: That was my next question. Why does Julia Roberts need me? Why does Donald Trump? I have written a book, *Step into the Spotlight!: 'Cause ALL Business is Show Business*. Why does Donald Trump need to be on the back of my book? He is already famous. Why would he care?

Jordan: They always have to stay in the spotlight. Why does he have to fight with Rosie O'Donnell?

Tsufit: Good point.

Jordan: He already has enough money but he knows it is going to keep his name up there. His TV show is *The Apprentice* and a new season is just starting. It is kind of ridiculous when you think these stars have so much money. If Madonna has so much money, why does she have to constantly be shocking?

Tsufit: Except the pope, yes.

Jordan: It keeps their name in the news. It gets someone on *Entertainment Tonight, Access Hollywood,* and CNN. It does not really matter how big they are. They still have to stay in the spotlight. Maybe you do not need Donald Trump but look at some other authors that are in the same field, these are still big names like Robert Kiyosaki or Suze Orman if you have a financial book. There are other authors that are going to want their name on the cover because that is going to refer people to their book is well. If you have done a book on dogs, maybe have, The Dog Whisperer. Someone that has been there…

Tsufit: I know there is a horse whisperer.

Jordan: Not the horse whisperer. I know it is someone that Oprah loves that trains the dogs.

Tsufit: I am not sure who that is.

Jordan: You want to stay in your field.

Tsufit: The other thing that makes sense is to find out what causes celebrities are interested in. If the person is a dog lover or working on seat belts for dogs or whatever they are working on, that would probably be an easier in too. Do you get that a lot?

Jordan: That is a great point. It is a lot easier to go after people that support a cause or a charity because they are already used to giving their support, so they want to support that cause. For instance, if you have written a book on dogs or animals, Betty White is a huge supporter of animals. She is still on TV but is mostly known for *Golden Girls.* She is not working as much, so she has more time to look over your manuscript and send a quote or a testimonial. Animals are something she is really passionate about. Go after stars that you know are interested in your cause. In our database that we have online, we actually list charitable causes.

Tsufit: That is fantastic.

Jordan: It is really great. You can select animals and it will give you a list of celebrities.

Tsufit: Really, by animal?

Jordan: Just animals.

Tsufit: Oh, animals. I say rabbit and you are going to tell me.

Jordan: That is a good idea. Maybe we should list it.

Tsufit: Yes. Gerbils.

Jordan: But most people that are interested in an animal are usually interested in…

Tsufit: All animals.

Jordan: Saving them.

Tsufit: Yes. It is the Bambi factor.

Jordan: Right. Maybe we should do that, like dogs.

Tsufit: You brought up another amazing point. You did not exactly highlight it but I think it is brilliant. You said Betty White is a little bit out of the spotlight right now so she has more time. I found this with books. I have been lucky enough to get some really amazing endorsements for my books mainly from marketing gurus, and people that are known in that regard, and authors.

I found it is easier to get somebody who is not on the bestseller list today but maybe they were on the bestseller list 10 years ago. Their name is just as hot. It might not be the most current name but some people have made their mark for the next hundred years based on previous work. They are not really that busy and sometimes, they even answer their own phone.

Jordan: We have an author who used our service. Her name was Jacqueline Marcell and she wrote a book called *Elder Rage*. She has written about her parents who both died of Alzheimer's and dementia. She was a first-time author that did not have any connections. After writing her book, she sent it out to probably a hundred celebrities and did exactly what you were saying. Jacqueline knew that probably, older people were going to be reading her book and knew she was not going to get Julia Roberts. Again, Julia Roberts is not going to help her book. So she sent it to people like Phyllis Diller and Bob Hope, this a few years ago but she sent it to people like that. A couple of them, I forgot the name, but he actually called her on the phone. I think it was Rod.

Tsufit: Rod Steiger. I heard about that. Yes.

Jordan: Right. He called her on the phone and said, "I cannot send you a quote. I am sick right now but please take it over the phone." He gave it to her and then, he died like a week later.

Tsufit: Oh. I got goose bumps just listening.

Jordan: I know.

Tsufit: And he did read it? He was a huge star before we were born.

Jordan: Right. And granted kids today probably do not know who Rod

Steiger is but the people today...

Tsufit: Today, they are not going to buy an Alzheimer's book, either.

Jordan: No. They are not. The people that are going to buy her book definitely know who he is. As we like to say it, a celebrity is a celebrity. If they were a celebrity 50 years ago, they are still a celebrity. It does not matter if they are still alive. It does not matter. Elvis is not alive.

Tsufit: I was going to say, "Can you put me in touch?" It is not that kind of a service, huh?

Jordan: I am not a psychic.

Tsufit: No séances or anything? Who qualifies as a celebrity? What kind of celebrities do you cover?

Jordan: We cover every person who is or was a celebrity. We do not really judge that much if you are a famous doctor, you are a celebrity.

Tsufit: Would I find a Nobel Prize winning scientist if I had written a book that this would be helpful for? Is it mostly movie stars?

Jordan: You would find Nobel Prize winners. You would find Olympians. We have most of the athletes. You would find artists, writers, photographers, and people like Annie Leibovitz, who is a famous photographer. She is a huge celebrity. She is not a movie star but we list people like that. This is a question we get asked a lot, do you just have movie stars? Yes, we have every movie star but then, we have a lot of other academic people as well including scientists. What else is there? There are politicians, world leaders, and religious figures.

Tsufit: Let me ask you, Jordan. If a person did not have access to your book or your service, which by the way, you should, it is fabulous. But let us say they did not for whatever reason. How would a person approach this on their own? Would it still be possible to get in touch with these celebrities on your own?

Jordan: It is definitely possible. The main thing is that it takes a lot more time.

Tsufit: How would you go about it if you wanted to track somebody down?

Jordan: Do you want to name somebody?

Tsufit: Well, Julia Roberts might be a bit hard. Let us just say I am a financial adviser and have written a book and I want somebody to endorse it.

Jordan: Okay. The first thing, it would help if you have a name but let us just say it is a financial person.

Tsufit: Well, let us say Suze. You said Suze Orman?

Jordan: Right. Suze Orman. The first step is…

Tsufit: Like how did she get to be Suze Orman? She probably went through a similar process, I imagine.

Jordan: Right. I am sure she did. I think she started out as a speaker. Actually, she started out as a stockbroker. Then she spoke and wrote books. I think she was smart and realized that the books were not what was going to make her rich. It was going to be speaking and selling products.

Tsufit: David Chilton is another stockbroker who wrote The Wealthy Barber. He is well known as well.

Jordan: And there is of course Martha Stewart. Stockbrokers must have this great luck at becoming famous. Okay, Suze Orman. Google is a great first step because you can find pretty much everything. Honestly, people think Google is so accurate. When we do research, we find that a lot of times, even the information they have on there is a little outdated. So you would look up Suze Orman. In her case, she is pretty easy because she has her own company or her publishing company. You basically want to find any kind of company that is associated.

We can use Martha Stewart. She has Martha Stewart Living, Omnimedia. She has a company, a publisher, an agent and managers. Usually, you can find that information on their official web site. Whatever celebrity it is if they have an official web site usually it lists their contact information. That is the easiest way. Movie stars and TV stars are a little harder because they are a little bit more private. So many people try and contact them that they do not want to really have that information out there.

Tsufit: Is it harder today to approach celebrities than it was before or is it easier? Which would you say?

Jordan: It is easier to find their information today, which is what the Internet with Google and services like ours do. I would say it is harder to actually make contact. We are living in this age right now where a celebrity is everything and there are so many magazines. *Star* and *Us Weekly* outsell *Time* and *Newsweek*.

Tsufit: Yes.

Jordan: You have everybody buying the celebrity tabloids. I have referred to it sometimes like an animal that has escaped from a zoo.

Everybody is fascinated and you want to get close to them but you cannot really. I do not know. It is just really hard right now to actually reach them because they have to be so careful. They have so many issues with people stalking them.

Tsufit: Yes. Let me ask you another question. Based on what you just said about their concern about stalking, what if you see a celebrity? Let us say you are at an event and you see them in the elevator, in the taxi, or backstage. Should you approach that person directly when you see them?

Jordan: If you say you are an author or you are a businessperson, I think it is okay. You want to be very polite. You do not want to intrude. I would not do it if they were eating dinner. Usually, they get upset or if they are in the bathroom. You know what they usually say in interview.

Tsufit: Oh, I have heard stories. Yes.

Jordan: Yes, they usually say they only get upset if they are eating or they are in the bathroom. I know it is kind of intimidating sometimes. Usually, they are pretty nice but you do not want to go up and just start talking to them about your book and go on and on. You might want to say I wrote a book and I would love to get in touch with your manager or your agent, can you tell me who it is? They will say call whatever the person's name is at CAA or whatever their agency is or they might give you a card. They are probably not going to sit there and talk to you for a long time but if you just want to get a quick piece of information, it is a great way.

If you see somebody at the airport rushing to their flight, it is really not a good time. If you are sitting next to them in first class, I have heard a lot of stories about people sitting next to a celebrity on a plane and talked about their book or handed them a copy because you always want to have your book with you.

Tsufit: Is flying first class just on the chance because you might?

Jordan: No. Although I have seen and read a lot of things about, when you fly, if you can afford it, you should because that is when people travel. You might be sitting next to Diane Sawyer and say "Oh, here is my book."

Tsufit: Especially maybe New York to LA, depending on the route.

Jordan: Right. That is true.

Tsufit: I mean if you are going to Iowa, maybe you could take economy. But you never know.

Jordan: Yes. You never know.

Tsufit: What do you do about nerves? This is something that I coach on but many people get really tongue-tied when they finally meet the celebrity of their dreams or they make contact by phone. All of a sudden, they do not even know their own name. What do you do about that? Does that ever happen to you?

Jordan: Oh, trust me, yes. It gets a little easier being in Hollywood because you see celebrities all the time. You see them without their makeup on. When I first moved there, it was funny because my mom would say, "Did you go to any parties or any premieres and see them?" I see them more at the drugstore and at the grocery store.

Tsufit: Really.

Jordan: It is funny because a lot of times, you will see them and say, "Do I know that person? Was it college? Was it high school?" You realize,

"Oh." It is someone that is on TV because they never look like they look on TV and do not look like they look in movies. They look like normal people. You realize these are normal people with not normal jobs.

Tsufit: You want to hear something funny? I was in a line at a conference and I was paying for biscotti and the woman in front of me, I said, "You look really familiar. Did we go to law school together?" I thought that is where I had met her. She said no but a lot of people say that. I was on *The Apprentice*. So, it is true. They are in our living room so we think we know them.

Jordan: Right. That is another part of it. They are in your living room on TV. In a way, in the back of your head you think, "Do I know that person?" especially when they are not dolled up and they do not have the makeup and the hair. They look like they could be your neighbor. When you live in those areas of the country like New York or LA, that they are regular people. There is nothing to really be scared about.

You see, on TV, where they are putting their hands up to the paparazzi and they are yelling at paparazzi and they are punching them sometimes but that is not how they are to their fans. They are normal people. There are these mobs of paparazzi, and they come at them with cameras. They know they are going to be on Entertainment Tonight that night looking like a normal person and not looking that great.

If you are a fan, it is great to just go up and say, "Hey. I love your work. By the way, I wrote a book. I would love to get it to you. What is the best way?" Just make it very short and again, tell them exactly what you want in a polite way. Usually, if somebody is rude to you, there is not much you can do about it. It is just a rude person having a bad day.

Tsufit: Let me ask you something. How do you know when to take no for an answer? I have heard some multi-million dollar best selling authors that say that no means not yet. On the other hand, you do not want to be perceived as a stalker. When do you quit? When do you take no for an answer?

Jordan: You definitely do not want to keep going if it is in person and the person says "No, not right now" or "I do not have time." You do not want to keep pressing because they probably do have security somewhere around.

Tsufit: Okay. So let us say it is not in person but let us say you have written or you have called and they said no a few times. Do you accept that or what do you do?

Jordan: No, you do not really accept it. You probably do not want to call back the next day but wait a week. Maybe call once a week and keep saying the same thing. With celebrities, it is true the nature of their jobs is they are not sitting in their office everyday like most people on their job. They are constantly traveling and working on new projects. They might be high for a year and extremely busy. The next year, they might not really have anything going on and they have more time so you do want to keep trying because their circumstances change so much. They absolutely have no time one day and then a few weeks later, they find themselves…

Tsufit: Between engagements?

Jordan: Right. Between engagements, wondering if they are going to have another movie or have a TV show. Or you are on a hot show this is an example, that show the *OC*. Well, that was a huge show. These people were extremely busy and now, that show is canceled and you wonder if they can…

Tsufit: Appear at the mall or something, giving out hotdogs.

Jordan: Right. Or are they going to be on anything as big.

Tsufit: It can happen.

Jordan: So you want to keep trying. I mean, those kids that were on *90210* when I was in high school? No time. Look at them now. Most of them are not really working.

Tsufit: Yes.

Jordan: You do not want to wait 10 years.

Tsufit: What did you say?

Jordan: They do not want to wait 10 years. That was a bad example.

Tsufit: Yes. You brought up another interesting point. You said that if you approach somebody one on one, they might give you a card and say contact so and so. That brings up the topic of the gateway people. I wonder if you can give us some tips for handling the lady in the horn-rimmed glasses. It is her job to keep you out. What is the best way to approach these really important people the gateway people? How do you know if you are being stalled?

Jordan: Having worked at these places, I can only share that you would not believe how many phone calls come in. When you call these people, many people are nervous and wonder all day long, am I going to call today? They call, and the person says, "What do you want? I cannot help you." Click.

You think, "Oh, my God, they were so rude to me. What did I do? I was just talking to them about my book." Having worked in these places, the phone does not stop ringing. Their bosses are yelling at them constantly because usually if you are calling, you are not going to be calling their home. We do not provide home phone numbers.

You are going to be calling their management company or agency and they represent a lot of other stars. It depends on how big the company is five to twenty agents may be working there. You are talking to an assistant who is answering the phone and he is to trying to handle a million other phone calls, that may not be more important to you but they are more important to the star or the agent about actual jobs.

They are very busy. I did not actually work at William Morris but I would go there to deliver things on my first job. They had at least ten people answering the phone. When you walked in, it was just like a boiler room operation but much nicer-looking. The phone was ring, ring on ten different desks with, "William Morris Agency" constantly.

You need to understand that you cannot call and start going into a long conversation. If you call and say, "Hi, I need to find out who represents this certain star?" They will tell you. If you call and say, I need to get something to this person. They will tell you but they are not even the ones that are going to be able to tell you whether the celebrity can endorse your book or not.

You really need to prepare package and send it in the mail and then wait and hear. If you do not hear anything back, keep sending it. Maybe keep calling, did they get the package? Am I sending it to the right person? Celebrities change representation a lot. Jennifer Lopez changed agencies 10 times in one year when she was first getting started. They will start out with the smaller agencies then suddenly become really famous and will switch to a bigger one, and they will be unhappy and switch to another one.

You really have to call and say, "Is she still represented by David so and so?" and they will say, "Yes, she is or No, she has changed. She is now with Endeavor. You can keep calling. You can keep bugging them but you want to do it in a way that is professional. "I am just making sure her information is still correct. I want to make sure I am sending this to the right place. Do I need to put anything special on the envelope to make sure it gets there?" You have to understand these people are so busy. If they are on the phone talking to an author about their work, "Oh, tell me about your book." They are not going to do that or hey are going to get fired, if they do.

Tsufit: Although if they do that, I would suggest that you do tell them rather than 'I want to talk to so and so', and you try to jump over them. One common complaint of the gateway people is that people do not realize that they are being asked to do that by the celebrity. We understand that but many people try to skip over the gateway people. I think that is probably a dangerous thing. Isn't it Jordan, to try to skip over them?

Jordan: Right. We get requests all the time. They say, "Can you just find me this person's home? You have to know where their home is and I would rather just send it to their home."

Tsufit: You might know but you cannot really release that, right?

Jordan: Right, even if you know. We do not release it because we do not want to be responsible for somebody doing something.

Tsufit: Yes.

Jordan: It is not the best way because when it goes to their home. We have all seen shows lately, especially all those reality shows about how they have assistants working at their homes. They are still going to have their mail screened.

Tsufit: Yes.

Jordan: If you send it to their management company or agency, they know where to locate that celebrity. Most of the celebrities have multiple homes. They are on location on different TV shows, different movies. For instance, the stars on Ugly Betty right now. I think the girl that plays *Ugly Betty* she goes to school at NYU.

Tsufit: America Ferrera.

Jordan: They shoot it in L.A. but also shoot at NYU. She is on both sides of the country, back and forth. Her agent or her manager is going to know where she is at the time. If you send it to her house, you do not know how long it is going to sit there.

Tsufit: Actually! Wouldn't she be a great person for a dentist or orthodontist to do something about braces? I am just looking for some weird tie-ins here.

Jordan: Exactly! You want to go after people that are related so you probably should not even waste your time. I do not want to say, do not reach for the stars but sometimes you just aim at people that are on TV. America Ferrera is probably just as busy as the huge stars right now but there are so many other people on that show or on shows like that.

Tsufit: How about the assistant guy? I forgot his name, the guy who plays the assistant to Wilhelmina. He would be fabulous for somebody that is training assistants or secretaries. I cannot even imagine right now what exactly you would do with that but he is such a personality. He is probably not the biggest target right now because he is not the star of the show. He might come out and speak to your group.

Jordan: Oh, definitely!

Tsufit: On Secretary's Day or whatever it is.

Jordan: Definitely. Especially, stars like that who are well-known but even if somebody does not recognize their name, you can still say, from *Ugly Betty*, so you can still use the TV show.

Tsufit: Sometimes they win awards too. When he does, then they can use that as well. I want to go back to what you were talking about the gateway people, this is just for authors right now. When I was getting endorsement for my book, sometimes I am speaking to an assistant and this happened over and over, I would notice that the assistant's last name was the same as the person I was trying to get. Sometimes, I would say, "Oh, are you any relation to …?" Oh yes, I am his daughter and I noticed the next time, I spoke to another assistant it was another daughter.

I have spoken to wives and to sons. These are really important gateway people that will influence in a big way, whether you get what you want or not. You have to be nice to them. I know somebody who is very successful and has built a huge business around befriending the gateway people.

Jordan: Definitely. You always want to be nice to them. It does not matter how rude they are.

Tsufit: He goes way beyond being nice and becomes their friend. Not in a using them kind of way. Even at a conference, when the big speaker is there, he does not necessarily go after trying to schmooze the big speaker. He goes to the back table because he knows that it is more likely that he will get there the other way.

Jordan: Right. That is a really good point. An insider secret, too, is you always want to be nice. Having worked there, I do not want to categorize all assistants and all people answering the phone as mean and rude. But having worked at three of them in different states, I can tell you it is pretty much the norm.

Tsufit: Were you mean and rude?

Jordan: No, not being rude like you would be rude to somebody that you know. They are being very matter-of-fact.

If you are nice and you keep calling and you are always nice to them. You remember their name and say, "Hi John! How are you? We spoke last week" but you still stay very succinct and to the point.

They will remember you and they are the ones that can do you a favor. They can walk right into their boss' office or when the celebrity comes in for meeting, they can say, "Hey, I got this. I think you should really look at it." They can do the biggest favors but they are only going to do a favor if you are nice. If you are a jerk to them and they will remember that too.

Tsufit: They will remember it for a hundred years when they move and work for someone else too.

Jordan: Right! Some of them work for smaller companies and smaller stars and they are going to talk to you a little bit more. They are going to be nice. For the bigger stars especially, they are just so busy but they will remember people that is part of their jobs to remember names.

If you are rude to them, they are going to remember you and they will probably not ever pay you any attention. You are definitely not going to get through. But they are treated usually, I do not want to say badly, but a lot of times badly by their bosses that when you are nice to them it really stands out. It stands out more than if you are calling a dentist office -- that is probably a bad example.

When you are calling a doctor's office, everybody is nice. Everybody is polite. "Hi, can I make an appointment?" But this is Hollywood and it is a different type of world where everybody is not so nice. It is very cutthroat and very competitive. If you are nice but still short and sweet and to the point, they are going to remember you and are going to be more likely to help you.

Tsufit: Jordan, I still have a lot of questions for you. But tell us first about your *Celebrity Black Book*. What is it?

Jordan: It is called the *Celebrity Black Book* (www.CelebrityBlackBook.com). We just came out with our 2007 edition. It contains the best mailing address for every celebrity we have in on our online database. For your listeners, it may be better for them to visit the website which is ContactAnyCelebrity.com because our online database has agents, managers, production companies and assistants with all our celebrities. The book has the best mailing address. If you are a non-profit, or work with an association, and you want to get autographs for an auction, the book is great. If you want to call the agents or managers, like we were just talking about, you probably want to go with the online database.

Tsufit: That is great to know. Let me ask you Jordan, "Do you know of anyone who has become a celebrity as a result of contacting celebrities?" I know this does not happen overnight. Can you think of any examples, not necessarily through your service but any people who have rubbed shoulders with celebrities and as a result ended up being celebrities themselves?

Jordan: I am not sure in terms of being on TV, although I am sure there are people. I am thinking professionally, like Jack Canfield, the *Chicken*

Soup books.

I was reading their books and when they first came out with their *Chicken Soup for the Soul* books, they were not famous, and had no connections. They bought a book of celebrity addresses just like our *Celebrity Black Book*. They sent their book out to people and wrote letters and started getting endorsements and testimonials. The story was actually a lot more exciting when I read it in their book.

Tsufit: They ended up on *Oprah*. Jack Canfield was just on *Oprah*. You are right, and I can think of a few other people. They may not be household names but you know Michael Budman who is one of the Roots guys. He is always hanging out with celebrities and he was making shoes.

Jordan: Yes.

Tsufit: I do not know if you saw a documentary called *My Date with Drew* about this guy who was down on his luck and did not have a lot of money, a regular Joe. Since he was a kid, he wanted to go out with Drew Barrymore. He launched this campaign and I will say borrowed, but actually he had a friend of his buy, a video camera. I am not sure if it was Best Buy or one of those stores. He had 30 days to return it because he could not really afford to keep it.

His goal was in 30 days to get a date with Drew Barrymore. It was very interesting how he went about doing that. I think he would have really been able to use your book because he went about it in a convoluted way. He is now a celebrity. I do not remember his name but he ended up getting a date with Drew. He has a documentary and has been on every TV show and news show. So, it does seem to work.

Jordan: I have one more quick story if you have time.

Tsufit: Yes, absolutely.

Jordan: It is in the new *Vanity Fair*. There was an interview with Brett Ratner. He is a very famous director. He is really young about 32 years old but he has directed *8 Mile* and a million music videos and movies with Chris Tucker and Chris Rock.

When he was in film school, he was making little student films and had no connections. He was writing to some directors asking if they would help support his movie. He wrote to 40 different ones and Steven Spielberg was the only one that wrote back and enclosed a check for a $1000.

Tsufit: Wow!

Jordan: I am not sure if they do that a lot or if something in his letter touched him. Years later, Steven Spielberg is at a party at his house. Lindsey Lohan and Paris Hilton are there because now he is friends with all these celebrities. When Steven Spielberg first met him he said, "Did you go to film school?" It is funny you should ask that because you sent me a check to fund my student film. He talks about when he was a kid on a plane he would go up and down the aisle talking to everybody, what do you do? How do you do it? Whenever he saw a celebrity on the street, he would go up and say, "Hi, I want to know you." He would approach celebrities in restaurants.

I am not saying that everybody should do this but you do have to be kind of pushy. Now he is one of the top directors and friends with every celebrity in Hollywood. Sometimes, it can work but you need a little luck on your side too.

Tsufit: Yes, a little bit of luck. You just cannot sit in your chair behind your desk because nobody is going to know that you exist.

Jordan: Right. You have to push. Everybody wants to be on *Oprah*. Getting on *Oprah* is hard but if you do not ever send her your book, or never send her a letter about your story, you are not going to get on *Oprah*. At least, you have to try.

Tsufit: There is a Canadian singer and he is not a household name yet, Ron Sexsmith. His fans are people like Elvis Costello and Paul McCartney, so that opens up a lot of doors. I think it was Samantha Marshall who certainly did not hurt her success when Elton John said he really was a fan. I hope I am getting these names right.

It certainly helps to be in the reflected light of a celebrity just to hang out with them. In fact it even works celebrity once or twice removed. I heard Jack Canfield speaking once and during the OJ trial, they sent *Chicken Soup* books to the jurors. They knew the jurors were bored at times. So they were filmed walking in and out of the courtroom with *Chicken Soup* books. That publicity did not hurt any either. Sometimes it is possible to be a pseudo celebrity. People do not necessarily know your name. When somebody dies and their obituary is on the Internet and it says veteran of 962 films and you do not know his name.

Jordan: Right.

Tsufit: That person is a celebrity and you could say that the star of so and so endorsed your film. There are so many ways to use this kind of information. I am thinking of our listeners who are primarily entrepreneurs, authors, and speakers.

What mistakes do people make with this information? I am not talking about using it for bad purposes, hopefully nobody would even think of doing that. If you have a good purpose, what are the mistakes that people should avoid?

Jordan: The first one is not matching the celebrity with their topic. It sounds like common sense but you would be surprised how many times people choose a celebrity that they love and watch on TV every night. "I would love to have so and so endorse my book" but they do not really stop and think, what does that celebrity have to do with my book and the topic?

Another one is not starting early enough. I keep using books but again with books, when you write a book, you have to send it out for reviews, three months before the book is even printed. You need those endorsements before you get the book printed. If the book is printed and then you start sending it out, you are going to have to wait until you reprint the book to put these endorsements on it. You want to send the manuscript to celebrities and try to get endorsements before the book is printed and done.

Another problem is people sending long letters and not really saying exactly what they want. Try to keep your letter to one page broken up and very easy to read. The person who is answering it should be able to just glance at it.

Tsufit: Some people have six pages of preamble about their organization.

Jordan: Yes.

Tsufit: If their request is on page seven, they are not going to get to page seven.

Jordan: Right, or they say we will keep it to one page but I will make the font really small and I will write a lot.

Tsufit: Yes.

Jordan: Keep it to a page. The point is so the person can easily see that they want an endorsement or an autograph.

Tsufit: Say in the first paragraph what is it you are going for?

Jordan: Exactly. Or put a post it note on the front that says, "I would love an endorsement. Thanks!" something very quick.

Another thing, especially for authors: write up the endorsements yourself and enclose a sheet that says here are some suggestions. Write three endorsements that you would want them to say and then just have a line with their signature and the date so they can say, "This one looks good! Yes, I would do that one." They can sign it and send it back to you.

So they do not have to sit there and think of one. Honestly, thinking of an endorsement, you might think it takes 2 seconds but for these people that are busy, they do not want to take the time to sit and think. First of all they have to read your book and a lot of them will flip through it and read a chapter; just basically to see if it looks good. Usually, they are not going to sit down unless they are very interested and read the entire thing cover to cover. If you can come up with three different quotes for them, and put them in where they can just sign off on it, that is really going to help.

Tsufit: Some people are going to hear what you are saying Jordan and think that is cheating. From my experience in contacting these people, they do want that. Even if they do not take your suggestion, it gives them an idea and they might take a word or sentence from each of the three and put it together. I know that is exactly what they want. That is fabulous advice.

Jordan, do you get people sending stories of their experiences contacting celebrities and what it did for them? What the results were?

Jordan: We get stories a lot and usually they are from entrepreneurs. I have a great one that is something everybody can use. We had a company that designs stuffed teddy bears in Australia. They would send the bears to celebrities that had just had children. We do not really recommend sending packages. There is nothing really wrong with sending a package, but if it gets lost or it does not get send back to you. Just know that you are not really in control of what happens to it because the assistant might think it looks great and take it home. Do not call us and complain that your package never got there.

Tsufit: Yes. Just to interrupt for one second.

Jordan: Sure.

Tsufit: I met a person who had a pin that she was promoting. Somebody told her to send it to Oprah. She said she already had and it got returned. I do not think they had even opened it.

Jordan: Yes, they may not even open them but do return them. Some places it might just disappear. If you send them a letter, you really do not lose anything. If you send a stuffed teddy bear, just know that it may get there or may not. They sent it to celebrities that have children. They received a handwritten note from Sarah Jessica Parker saying, "My child loves this bear. She sleeps with it every night. Thank you so much. Thank you for thinking of me. It is so cute and cuddly." This is not a famous company like Mattel. This is a husband and wife that design these bears from their home. They are a very small company, and they are trying to get their name launched. They are not famous yet. They took that thank you note and put in on their website.

In their marketing materials it said Sarah Jessica Parker loves this bear, "I love this bear! Sarah Jessica Parker." Everybody knows Sarah Jessica

Parker. They were lucky they had a Thank You note from a huge star. It really helped boost their sales and it got the attention of distributors and stores. Things like that really do help.

Someone faxed us yesterday with a similar thing. They had sent something to Dakota Fanning. Dakota Fanning wrote back in her handwriting, "Thank you so much! I love the …" I cannot remember what the product was but it says, "I love this, it is so cute!" They can do the same thing and use that Thank you note on their website.

Tsufit: Let me ask you. Is there a protocol around that? Do they need to ask for permission to use it?

Jordan: It is sort of your comfort level. You are right.

Tsufit: Personally, I would want to make sure that it was okay because I have been quoted in newspapers from private emails that I sent.

Jordan: Right.

Tsufit: I was intending to just send it to an editor as a thank you or something like that. I would err on the side of caution just making sure it is okay. If you do want to make sure that you get an answer back, you could send a one-line e-mail that says, "I am intending to use this. Thank you so much. If there is any problem, please let me know." If they do not let you know, it kind of changes the onus that you could go ahead and do it. What do you think about that?

Jordan: You are right. I think that brings up a good point. I would enclose, when they sent the bear to Sarah Jessica Parker, I am not sure if they did or not, but in the letter saying, we would appreciate a note back…

Tsufit: That we could use maybe in our materials or something.

Jordan: Yes. You would have to think of a way to do that. I am not sure if they did that or not. These are not normal people they deal with this everyday.

Tsufit: That is true.

Jordan: A lot of celebrities know that if I send this company a thank you note, it is going end up in their marketing. It is going to end up on their website.

Tsufit: You are right. That is a very good point because their face ends up all over the place without them…

Jordan: It is publicity for them in way if this company becomes big saying Sarah Jessica Parker loves it. You read all the time in Us Weekly where people will talk about tons of different products that celebrities use like beauty products and they will say so and so loves. So and so came into my store and she loved this dress. I do not know if they ever got permission to say that to Us Weekly or to say that in their marketing? They just assumed.

Tsufit: The truth is, do they get permission to put people on the worst dressed list in People magazine? Probably not either, so I guess you are right. Once you are in that arena, all is fair. I was reading in your materials that somebody had sent some designer clothing to Goldie Hawn and was it Patricia Arquette? They got a nice note about their Cabo San Lucas Store.

Jordan: Right. We have a lot people who do this. In your head, you think that it is really going to be hard to do but we hear from a lot of people. We had someone with a scarf company that did a campaign to celebrities and got Thank You notes back.

Tsufit: Yes. You could put a picture, not necessarily a picture wearing this thing. Although it would be nice if you could say, could you please send us a picture wearing it? Even if you did not have that, if you put a picture of the celebrity on your website or in your store, or in your marketing materials with a quote right underneath it. It almost feels like that they sent it to you with the picture. It really stands out and looks like a really solid endorsement.

Jordan, how do you use celebrities to promote your business and your book? Or have you?

Jordan: Yes, we have done it a little bit. For instance, I got to meet Perez Hilton, a few weeks ago…

Tsufit: So how is Paris doing?

Jordan: It was not Paris Hilton the blonde girl. It was Perez Hilton who a lot of people may not know. I was just watching *The View* this morning and Rosie O'Donnell was talking about him. He is a gossip blogger on the Internet and he writes a daily blog about celebrity gossip. He has four million people a day look at it. A lot of people know who he is. I think Rosie has mentioned him two to three times on *The View*, Oprah has mentioned him. He is the new gossip magazine.

Tsufit: Right.

Jordan: I met him and made sure that I got a picture with him. He is the celebrity kind of guru right now. We have just put that picture up on our My Space page. We have a ContactAnyCelebrity.com My Space page, since we want to keep up with the technology. We will put him on there because you can put photos up there. It will also be on our website.

Tsufit: When you meet a celebrity, should you approach him on the street and get a photo with them?

Jordan: If you go to a seminar or trade show and they have a celebrity speaker, try to get a photo with them.

Tsufit: That is brilliant advice. Actually, Mark Victor Hansen really promotes that very heavily. I have a picture with him that I have not used yet. Mark says that if you go to a conference, get a picture with every speaker there. Then later if you get a little blurb from them, imagine you can put up a picture of you and them, the blurb and it has so much weight.

So how do use it to promote yourself?

Jordan: That is a great point. I never really did this until recently. We go to marketing seminars all the time. You usually have someone that is pretty well known to get a picture with and you can use in on your website. If you are an entrepreneur and you get a picture with Donald Trump if he is speaking or whoever else, use that on your website. This makes you look more credible and like you know what you are doing and more of an expert.

Tsufit: Have you got any endorsements for your book?

Jordan: For the *Celebrity Black Book* it is tough. We have a new book coming out called *Secrets to Contacting Celebrities* and I actually have sent it off to some people that are gossip columnists. A book that just came out on the bestseller list is called *Fame Junkies*. It is about why people are obsessed with celebrities and why they are obsessed with fame. It is a really good book if anyone wants to read it by Jake Halpern. I looked up his website and e-mailed him and said we are coming out of this book, Could I submit it to you? He wrote back, and said "Yes, I would love to read it. I would love to give you a quote if I like it." So then we would put on the cover whatever quote he says, Jake Halpern, the author of *Fame Junkies*...

Tsufit: Yes, that is perfect.

Jordan: That is good publicity for him.

Tsufit: Yes, that is exactly what you said at the outset about matching. For example, if you did get Julia Roberts to endorse your book, what does that really say? I do not know that it would really be more like the guy you talked about. I see that you do have a few endorsements from Hollywood insiders or people in agencies, or people who need this information or said that they could have used it years ago when they were doing whatever they were doing, when they had to find celebrities. You are right if you do not match it properly, people are going to be reading it and say, so what if John Travolta thinks you have a good list of celebrities.

Jordan: Right. We have had more success with the *Celebrity Black Book* sending it to get reviews on magazines and trade publications. It is not a book. It is more of a directory.

Tsufit: Yes.

Jordan: Books that you are coming out with are a little easier, Things that we can actually read and skim through. People do not really want to endorse directories that much.

Tsufit: Yes. Jordan, this has been absolutely fabulous. As I said our listeners are basically entrepreneurs, authors and speakers who really want to standout and get noticed. I think you have spelled out a perfect plan for almost anybody to make his or her way into the spotlight to help them get noticed. Any really unique approach you have seen or heard? We have heard about people who rented the football stadium, what is that when they fly a hot air balloon and have a streamer following the hot air balloon? Any kind of unique celebrity stories that we can end on today or if not just any last tips?

Jordan: I have a tip that I thought of which if any of your listeners are in fashion or they design jewelry or any product…

Tsufit: My daughter makes jewelry, so bring it on, and let me tell her. What should she do?

Jordan: We have a customer who designs inspirational jewelry from home. She is trying to get launched so she sent it to all of these wardrobe people on TV shows. She heard back from the person in-charge that made wardrobe for *The OC* and she loved it. She outfitted four or five of the main girls on the TV show with this jewelry. She can say "as seen on *The OC.*"

Someone saw it on The OC from Amazon, and thought this would be great to have on Amazon. They created a whole little mini store on Amazon of this inspirational jewelry as seen on The OC by this woman. Her sales totally escalated. That was a great idea sending to it wardrobe. Now all you have to do it find who the production company is for the TV show. There are tons of TV shows. Just call them up and say, "What is the name of the person that does wardrobe on your show?" When you watch Ugly Betty there is that woman that does all the clothes…

Tsufit: Yes, Christina.

Jordan: Yes, usually somebody like that or one or two people. Send it to wardrobe people on TV shows and then there is whole another thing, which is too complex, maybe you can have me back for another show.

Tsufit: Yes, absolutely.

Jordan: Product placement is great. There are a lot of TV shows. I keep using *Ugly Betty* just because I have gotten an e-mail from them about once a day, looking for products to be on the show. They are looking for everything from expensive stuff like a motorcycle to inexpensive stuff like mens' hats. We are looking for soap or bath products. You think these shows have tons of money but it is hard to believe but strict budgets…

Tsufit: So you could be helping them too.

Jordan: They want to get as much stuff as they can for free. They do not want to go out and buy tons of bath products for one little bathtub scene where Wilhelmina is sitting in the bathtub and you see these products around her.

Tsufit: Wow, so that is a scoop. If you make soap or anything like that, you just send it to them. Jordan, that is actually a fabulous thing that we were not really talking about until now. This is brilliant that you do not just have to contact the celebrities.

Jordan: Yes.

Tsufit: It could be the behind the scenes people and get placement and then you become the celebrity, which is the whole point of our show. The show is *Secrets from the Spotlight*. Our guest has been Jordan McAuley. He is from ContactAnyCelebrity.com. He has a fabulous *Celebrity Black Book* at www.CelebrityBlackBook.com and is a reservoir of information not only on how to contact celebrities but why and how to do it.

I am Tsufit from *Secrets from the Spotlight* at www.SecretsFromTheSpotlight.com. I want to thank you Jordan.

Additional Resources

Books by Jordan McAuley

The Celebrity Black Book
Over 55,000 Accurate Celebrity Addresses for Fans, Businesses and Nonprofits
www.CelebrityBlackBook.com

Secrets to Contacting Celebrities
101 Ways to Reach the Rich and Famous
www.SecretsToContactingCelebrities.com

Databases

Celebrity Causes Database
www.CelebCauses.com

Contact Any Celebrity
www.ContactAnyCelebrity.com

Toolkits

Celebrity Book Endorsements Toolkit
www.BookEndorsements.com

How to Hire a Celebrity
www.HowToHireACelebrity.com

Make Your Book Famous
www.MakeYourBookFamous.com